Suli's Big Race

by Alex Eeles
illustrated by Alan Rogers

Little Suli the elephant liked to run.
She had little legs
and a round tummy.

She did not run fast.

Taz the cheetah liked to run, too.
He had long legs. He ran fast.

Suli wanted to run fast like Taz.
The animals laughed at her.

'Slowcoach Suli,' they said.

Suli was sad.
She wanted to run fast, too.

One day, Taz said,
'Let's have a race.'

'Okay,' said Suli. 'I will win.
I will get to that big tree
before you.'

Everyone laughed.

'Slowcoach Suli,' said Taz.

They started to run.

They ran across the long grass.
Suli ran, but Taz ran
faster and faster.

'I must keep going,' said Suli.

Suli came to some big rocks.
'Oh no!' she said.

She looked up and saw Taz
near the big tree.

'I must keep going,' she said.

Taz looked at Suli
and the two big rocks.

'Slowcoach Suli,' he laughed.

But Taz did not see the wet mud and he ran into it.

'Help me,' he shouted.
'I am stuck.'

But Suli loved the mud
and ran past him.

Suli got to the big tree.

'Suli is the winner,' said the animals.

'She kept going all the way
to the tree.'

All the animals cheered.

And no one called Suli
a slowcoach ever again.

Suli's Big Race 🐾 Alex Eeles

Teaching notes written by Sue Bodman and Glen Franklin

Using this book

Developing reading comprehension

This story is an innovation on the fable of the Tortoise and the Hare. Suli the Elephant liked to run but could not run fast. One day, Taz the Cheetah challenged her to a race. Children will be able to make links with their own experiences and with other stories in which the underdog triumphs in the end. Suli is not an object of ridicule but an example of how strong character and tenacity are admirable personal qualities. See also 'The Lion and The Mouse' (Green band in the Cambridge Reading Adventures) for another retelling of a traditional fable.

Grammar and sentence structure

- Some use of literary language ('*One day*') and repeated phrases ('*I must keep going!*').
- Speech punctuation serves to track continued dialogue after the reporting clause, such as on page 14.
- Both regular past tense verbs with /ed/ inflections and irregular past tense verbs ('*ran*', '*came*') are featured.

Word meaning and spelling

- Adjectives describe appearance and add to character description: '*long grass*', '*little legs*', '*big rocks*'.
- The level of challenge provides opportunity for children to decode single syllable CVC words fluently using their growing phonic knowledge.

Curriculum links

PE – Children will be familiar with races and school sports. Set up an obstacle course for a class race (but perhaps not with mud!)

PSHE – Running is one way of keeping fit. The text would support work on health, well-being and exercise.

Learning Outcomes

Children can:

- read aloud demonstrating appropriate pace and emphasis
- comment on events and characters, using the text to support their opinions
- decode single syllable words using their phonic knowledge, with fast visual recall of known high frequency words.

A guided reading lesson

Book Introduction

Activate children's prior knowledge by discussing events such as a recent PE lesson, sports day or national/intentional athletic events. Give each child a copy of the book. Read the title and the blurb.

Orientation

Give a brief overview of the story, using the same verb tense as used in the book, *Suli the Elephant liked to run, but she did not run fast. One day, she had a race with Taz the Cheetah. Who do you think will win?*

Preparation

Pages 2 and 3: *Here are Suli and Taz. Can you find Suli's name? Read along the word with your finger and say her name slowly. Now find the word 'Taz' on page 3. Read along the word and say his name slowly. How do we know Taz will be able to run fast? Yes, it says he has 'long legs'. How does the author describe Suli's legs? Show me on page 2. Hmmm, yes – she has little legs. Look at this last line: 'She did not run fast'.*

Page 4: Look at the two-syllable word '*Slowcoach*' and explain the meaning for children unfamiliar with the word. It is important to support this as the word occurs several times in the story.